Lighting Designer
Kathrine Sandys

Spanning scenography, installation, research, education, publication and curation, Kathrine has worked predominantly with light and sound in live performance, installation, museum display, site-specific events and research through reimagined landscapes – industrial and military.

She was recipient of the "International Award for Excellence in Sound Design" for Hush House, at the 2011 Prague Quadrennial.

International commissions have included collaborations in Czech Republic, South Africa, India, Japan, Philadelphia, Ireland, Ghana, NY ICFF, Harare International Festival of Arts, Prague Quadrennial and the International Dance Collective (IcoDaCo). UK commissions have included Aldeburgh Music; Liverpool Theatres (Everyman, Playhouse, Unity); Imperial War Museum North and Churchill War Rooms; Opera North; Liverpool International Biennial of Contemporary Art; Vintage at Goodwood; Royal Liverpool Philharmonic Orchestra; FACT; East Midlands Cultural Olympiad 2012 and Tate Liverpool.

Sound Designer
Frazer Merrick

Frazer is a sound artist who uses field recording, circuit bending and instrument building to create carnivalesque sonic experiences. Frazer's work is curious, interactive and collaborative.

He's played a gig underwater, made a banana piano and is currently building the Photon Smasher, a microphone for listening to light.

His score for **Sirens** was composed from recordings made around Mersea Island, with the sounds of Cudmore Grove, oyster fisheries and boat yards all sampled and woven into the soundtrack.

I0203494

Your theatre, your stories

The Mercury is an artistic powerhouse in the East - a vital vibrant, welcoming centre of culture for the people of Colchester, Essex and beyond.

The theatre takes its name from the Roman messenger god, Mercury. It was Mercury's task to connect the people with the gods, and so, in keeping with our name, connection is at the heart of everything we do.

We connect through the live event, the shared experience. The award-winning theatre that we present electrifies, transforms and enriches the lives of our community. We reinvent old stories and conjure up bold, new ones. Stories that reach out and touch our audience, stories from fresh voices that demand to be heard.

We connect with the diverse communities that surround us through our participation programmes, which celebrate creative potential by providing people with everyday opportunities to be artistic and innovative.

We connect by putting inclusivity, accessibility and empowerment at the centre of all our work.

We connect with the wider theatre industry and have been nominated for 15 different national awards over the last three years for our productions of **Pieces of String, Noughts and Crosses, Ain't Misbehavin', Cinderella** and our work in the community. We are proud to have won four of these awards; especially the UK Theatre Award for Excellence in Inclusivity.

After an unprecedented year where we connected with our audiences and local creatives online, we re-opened our new-look building in Summer 2021 and welcomed audiences back with our madcap comedy **Baskerville**. We have launched our Taking Part activities offering creative classes for all and our café bar is open all day for coffee, tea and a whole range of treats. We hope you'll agree, the Mercury is more than a great night out. It's where we connect.

Author's Note

Someone asked me recently why I wrote this play. It's one of those funny questions you get asked from time to time. I rattled off talk of themes. The characters. The world of the play. The usual stuff. But really there's a lot more to it than that.

Thirteen years ago when I was just starting out as a playwright I sent a letter to the Mercury Theatre asking if someone would meet me to have a chat. Tony Casement (the Associate Director) wrote back and said to come in for a coffee…. And for the first time I got to feel like I was actually a writer. Things like that matter. The idea, for a kid from Thurrock, that someone is interested in them. That someone thinks it might be a good idea to carry on rather than give up.

A lot of time has passed since then. The grey hair gives it away. I've been lucky to carve out a career in writing. I'll spare you the CV, but amongst it all I've always maintained a great relationship with the Mercury. I've had a couple of plays tour here and adapted **Quadrophenia** for their young company. I teach their writers programme bringing through new voices from the Eastern region. And now **Sirens** gets to be the first in a series of plays titled Mercury Originals going on in their newly refurbished studio theatre.

None of that happens without that cup of coffee thirteen years ago.

So in truth, that's why I wrote this play. Because someone made time in their day to meet me. To make me believe that I could be a writer. And for that I'll always be eternally grateful.

Kenny Emson

Foreword from the Mercury

The Mercury is an artistic engine room in the East of England – a vital, vibrant, welcoming centre of culture for the people of Colchester, Essex and beyond. We exist to push the boundaries of theatre and its form by collaborating with exceptional people who enrich and diversify the narratives, practices and voices of the UK's theatre ecology.

Each year we programme a range of risk-taking, compelling new works in our studio theatre known as Mercury Originals. These plays are nurtured through the Mercury's artist development programme, which aims to cultivate the theatre makers of tomorrow by seeking out our region's boldest, most theatrically-daring artists and providing them with the support and space to explore and test their ideas. This includes commissions, research and development weeks, artists in residence, and ongoing investment through extended sector collaboration to create new works.

We are delighted that our inaugural Mercury Original is **Sirens** by Kenny Emson, a playwright from Thurrock writing about the Essex experience.

Sirens was made possible at the Mercury with the support of SELEP Ltd as part of Catalyst For Culture in partnership with Marlowe Theatre.

To find out more about the Mercury please visit mercurytheatre.co.uk

Ryan McBryde
Creative Director, Mercury Theatre

Meet the Team

Directors

Ir Lyn Barton
amantha Blackwell-Heard
athleen Hamilton (Chair)
yan Johnston
assina Khan
atthew Linley

Sean Plummer (Treasurer)
Patrick Sandford
Jennie Skingsley
Anita Thornberry
Simon Warwick
Rob West (Vice Chair)

Executive

Executive Director Steve Mannix
Executive Producer Tracey Childs
Creative Director Ryan McBryde
Deputy Executive Director Deborah Sawyerr

Production

Head of Construction Phillip Attwater
Production Manager Richard Parr
Technical Manager Ben Wills
Company Stage Manager Rebecca Samuels
Wardrobe Manager Corinna Vincent
Production Administrator Jenny Moore
Stage One Producer Placement Jess Donn

Workshop

Deputy Workshop Manager Harriet Wheatley
Workshop Assistant (Maternity Cover) Jim Bonner

Wardrobe

Deputy Wardrobe Manager Chantelle Cox

Technical

Senior Technician (Stage) Roger Mills Lewis
Technicians Wesley Laing, Caitilin Pegley, Darryl Ward

Development

Head of Development Abigail Roberts

Creative Engagement

Mercury Creatives Project Manager Joseph Rawlings
Mercury Creatives Project Coordinator Elodie Gilbert
Head of Creative Engagement Laura Norman
Talent Development Producer Dilek Latif
Creative Engagement Administrator Forest Morgan
Talent Development Administrator Anna Bolton

MYC Youth Assistants:
Molly Featherstone, Thomas Grubb, Rhys Lifton, Eilish Mullane, Theodore Roper, Koralia Salacuri

Marketing

Interim Head of Marketing & Communications Sue Lawther-Brown
Senior Marketing Officer Rhianna Howard
Marketing & Data Management Officer Emily Carter

Operations

Operations Director Carol Rayner
Facilities & Projects Manager Nik Frampton
Theatre Administrator Valentina Borja Herrera
Theatre Administrator (Maternity Cover) Lorena Saiano
Administration Assistant Jack Pedersen
Cleaning Supervisor Edward Cleary
Head Chef Daniel Collins
Line Chef Andrew Tulloch
Kitchen Assistants David Attan, Ellianna Stewart

Finance

Finance Director Hazel Skayman
Finance Officer Kristin Green
Finance Officer Fiona Lucas

Customer Experience

Customer Experience Supervisors:
Oliver Harrington, Annaleise Sansum, Emma Vidler

Interim Customer Experience Supervisors:
Stefan Davies-Capper

Customer Experience Assistants:
Jessica Ashley, Aleksandra Astrauskaite, Rush Atherton, James Bacon, Richard Bland, Anita Cadogan, Emanie Cherry, Justin Eade, Rachael Fontenelle, Clarissa Hankin, Georgina Hart, Irsan Ismail, Megan Juniper, Kelly Koreman-Ball, September Mead-Smith, Sarah Mills, Jonathan Moran, Veronica Morris, Oliva Ochaya, Kylise Palmer, Maria Rutherford

Customer Experience Trainees:
Summer Crosby, Kieron Gould, Caitlin Hegarty, Connor Hickman, James Maddison, Chantel Morrison, Drew Pasmore, Leonard Shannon-Bright, Chloe Smith, Jack Smith

SIRENS

CAST

Rory Simon Darwen
Gemma Tanya-Loretta Dee
Isla Jesse Akele

CREATIVES

Writer Kenny Emson
Director Bethany Pitts
Co-Designer Cara Evans
Co-Designer Zoë Hurwitz
Lighting Designer Kathrine Sandy
Sound Designer Frazer Merrick
Intimacy Director Louise Kempton
Voice and Accent Coach
Katherine Heath

PRODUCTION MANAGEMENT

Producer Dilek Latif
Production Manager Richard Parr
Production Administrator Jenny Moore
Stage One Producer Placement Jess Donn

WORKSHOP

Head of Construction Phillip Attwater
Deputy Workshop Manager Harriet Wheatley
Scenic Carpenter Rob van der Parker
Workshop Assistant (Maternity Cover) Jim Bonner
Scenic Artists Rhiannan Howell, David Thomas

WARDROBE

Costume Supervisor Angela Whatling
Wardrobe Manager Corinna Vincent
Assistant Costume Supervisor Chantelle Cox
Wardrobe Assistant Lucinda Cawdron, Jess Fisher

STAGE MANAGEMENT

Company Stage Manager Rebecca Samuels
Deputy Stage Manager Lucy Quinton
Assistant Stage Managers Gillian McGrath

TECHNICAL

Senior Stage Roger Mills Lewis
Techincal Stage Darryl Ward
Production Lighting Caitilin Pegley
Production Sound Wesley Laing

MARKETING

Photograhy Pamela Raith
National PR Kate Morley PR
Marketing Lead Emily Carter

CAST

esse Akele
a

sse was raised in Bradford before moving to
ndon to join the LAMDA foundation course.
e then went on to study on the BA Acting course
East15 where she played such roles as: Annie in
uswell Hill, Lady Capulet in **Romeo and Juliet** and
iel in **The Pillowman**.

hile at East15 she was also the receiver of the
urence Olivier Bursary Award.

nce graduating in 2018 her credits include: **Under
ater Love** (Futures Theatre Company); **The
nnatural Tragedy** (The White Bear); **Bare** (Raindog
ms); **There Are No Beginnings** (Leeds Playhouse).
her spare time Jesse is also a portrait artist.

anya-Loretta Dee
Gemma

anya-Loretta Dee is an actor and writer. She
cently appeared in Acorn TV's **Whitstable Pearl**,
nd is due to appear in Season 6 of **Peaky Blinders**
2022. She played semi-regular character DS
argrave in BBC **Doctors**, and currently plays
gular character PC Olsen in the BBC One soap
astenders. Recent theatre credits include working
ith MiddleChild Theatre in Paines Plough
oundabout on **One Life Stand**. Tanya was
ominated for a West End Offie for her portrayal of
illow in **Boots** (The Bunker Theatre), and she
arred as Jane, in the Willy Russell play **One for the
oad** (Frinton Repertory Theatre).

Simon Darwen
Rory

Theatre credits include: **Beginning** (Queens
theatre Hornchurch/Theatre Royal Bath/National
Theatre); **Missing People** (Leeds
Playhouse/National Theatre Tokyo); **Skellig**
(Nottingham Playhouse); **Much Ado About
Nothing** (Jamie Hendry
Productions/NESC/International Tour); **The Here
and This and Now** (Plymouth Drum/Southwark
Playhouse); **The Pitmen Painters** (New Vic); **Our
Country's Good** (Out of Joint); **Lizzie Siddal**
(Arcola); **The Armour/Hotel Plays** (Defibrilator);
Flare Path (National Tour); **Catch 22** (Northern
Stage); **Virgin** (Watford Palace); **King Lear**
(Theatre Royal Bath); **Mad About The Boy** (Young
Vic/Bush Theatre); **Sour Lips** (Oval House); **The
Fifth Column, The Taming of the Shrew, What
the Women Did** (Southwark Playhouse); **Love
Love Love** (Original Cast) (Paines Plough);
Unrestless (Old Vic Tunnels); **Accolade** (Original
Revival Cast) (Finborough Theatre); **Ramshackle
Heart** (Public Theatre New York); **Arse, Shove**
(Theatre 503); **Mad Forest, The Wonder** (BAC); **The
Merchant of Venice, The Tragedy of Thomas
Hobbes, The Taming of the Shrew, A Midsummer
Night's Dream** (RSC); **Fanny & Faggot** (Trafalgar
Studios); **Nikolina, Bedtime for Bastards**
(nabokov).
Television credits include: **Years and Years;
Britannia; Call the Midwife; Silent Witness; The
Bletchley Circle; The Bill.**
Simon has also recorded numerous audiobooks.

CREATIVES

Writer
Kenny Emson

Kenny Emson is an award winning, and BAFTA nominated, writer for stage and screen.

His plays include: **Terrorism** (Bush Theatre); **Plastic** (ORL and Mercury Theatre); **Rust** (Hightide and Bush Theatre); **Parkway Dreams** (Eastern Angles); **Our Nobby** (Eastern Angles); **Quadrophenia** (Mercury Theatre); **Misfits** (Queens Theatre Hornchurch).

Director
Bethany Pitts

Bethany Pitts is an award-winning theatre director who trained on the National Theatre Studio Directors Course and as an Assistant Director at Theatre Royal Plymouth and Theatre 503.

Directing credits include: **Juniper and Jules** by Stephanie Martin (Soho Theatre/VAULT Festival - Show of the Week Award); **Fuck You Pay Me** by Joana Nastari (VAULT & Edinburgh Festivals/Bunker Theatre); **A Funny Thing Happened On The Way To The Gynecologic Oncology Unit** by Halley Feiffer (Finborough Theatre, UK premiere – 3 x Off West End Nominations); **3 Billion Seconds** by Maud Dromgoole (VAULT/Paines Plough Roundabout); **Brutal Cessation** by Milly Thomas (Assembly Edinburgh/Theatre 503); **Spine** (Underbelly Edinburgh/Soho Theatre/UK Tour – Fringe First Winner); **Tether** (Underbelly Edinburgh); **FreeFall** by Vinay Patel (Pleasance Islington – Nominated for Off West End Best Director); **DESERT** (National Tour/Latitude Festival).

Assistant/Associate directing includes: **Song At Twilight** by Noel Coward (Theatre Royal Bath); **Abi** by Athia Sen Gupta (Derby Theatre/Queens' Theatre Hornchurch); **Frogman** by curious directive (Shoreditch Town Hall/Norwich Theatre Royal/UK Tour); **Dark Vanilla Jungle** by Philip Ridley (Soho/Pleasance - Fringe First winner); **Theatre Uncut** (Traverse Theatre Fringe First Winner/Young Vic).

Co-Designer
Cara Evans

Cara is a performance designer working primarily within theatre and film. They trained in Design for Stage at RCSSD and Fine Art at UCA.

They are an associate artist at OPIA Collective and have worked as a reader at the Royal Court Theatre.

They recently designed: **Living Newspaper** (Royal Court) as part of a design collective; **Ordinary Miracle** (NYT); **The Girl with Glitte in her Eye** (Bunker); **Refuge** and **The Woman Who Turned Into a Tree** (New Nordics Festival); and co-designed **Queer Upstairs** (Royal Court).

They have worked as an associate for Naom Dawson and Chloe Lamford, most recently c Donmar Warehouse's School's Tour of **Teenage Dick**. They have also worked as an assistant for Rosanna Vize, Fly Davis and Sophie Jump.

Co-Designer
Zoë Hurwitz

Zoë is a London based designer originally from Essex.

Most recent UK credits include: **Malindadzin** (Hampstead Theatre); **Deciphering** (New Diorama - Off West End Award nominee best Set Design 2021); **The Language of Kindness** (Shoreditch Town Hall); **Fen** (LAMDA); **We Anchor in Hope** (Bunker); **The Five Plays Project** (Directors Programme, Young Vic); and as designer for the Living Newspaper collective at the Royal Court.

Recently working in New York, she has designed for US venues such as Here Arts Center, Ars Nova (AntFest); The Wild Project, and Brown/Trinity Rep.

Selected production design credits include: **Assisted Living** (web series, NYC); **Pear** (mus video, NYC); **La Tercera Llamada** (short, Mexico).

Recent assistant credits include: **Caroline or Change** (Fly Davi at Studio 54 NYC); **Social!** (Christine Jones at the Park Avenue Armory); **Constellations** (Tom Scutt at the Vaudeville).

Zoë was a winner of the 2019 Linbury Prize for Nuffield Southampton and a finalist in the 2020 JMK award designing for Emerald Crankson. She was a finalist in the 2015 Off West End Awards for **Lovesong of the Electri Bear** (Hope Theatre/The Arts Theatre) and a Jerwood Assistant Designer at the Gate Theatre.

She completed an MFA in Design at New York University in 2019, and holds a BA in Fine Art from Chelsea School of Art. London. www.zoehurwitz.com

Kenny Emson

Sirens

Salamander Street

PLAYS

First published in 2021 by Salamander Street Ltd.
(info@salamanderstreet.com)

Sirens © Kenny Emson, 2021

ISBN: 9781914228520

10 9 8 7 6 5 4 3 2 1

For my brother

A saver of lives. And a drinker of pints.

Acknowledgements

Thanks to… Ryan, Dilek, Tracey, Steve and the rest of the team at the Mercury. Nish, Sam and Adam at Curtis Brown. George at Salamander Street. Declan Feenan and the bais. And, as ever, Ange… for putting up with me.

KE.

Cast

1

RORY, *Seventeen*

GEMMA, *Seventeen*

2

RORY, *Thirty-Four*

ISLA, *Seventeen*

3

RORY, *Fifty-one*

GEMMA, *Fifty-one*

1.

The RNLI station. Mersea Island. Night. Autumn.

GEMMA, *seventeen, enters sheepishly with a torch. She whispers:*

GEMMA: Rory?

> *She moves around with the torch. We get glimpses of the RNLI lifeboat in the background. Various life jackets hung up on the walls.*

Rory...

> *The torch homes in on a bottle of wine sat on the floor in front of the boat. A couple of unlit candles next to it.*

I know you're here.

Pause.

Is this meant to be funny or something?

Pause.

Oh, where is Rory? Should I ring the police? Maybe he's been kidnapped by aliens looking to run tests on lifeforms with tiny brains and even smaller –

> **RORY**, *also seventeen, hops out of a life jacket cupboard to the side of* **GEMMA** *making her jump out of her skin.*

You are such a prick.

RORY: But an above average sized one.

GEMMA: I'm going home.

RORY: You're not going home.

GEMMA: I am.

RORY: I bought wine.

GEMMA: I'm not drinking.

RORY: Of course you are. It's Friday night. Everyone's fucking drinking. What else is there to do?

GEMMA: Go down The Victory. Be with some normal people.

RORY: Normal people?

GEMMA: Yeah.

RORY: How many normal people do you know round here?

GEMMA: Loads. Present company excluded.

RORY: Normal people are boring people.

GEMMA: Boring is better than being a prick.

RORY: Says who?

GEMMA: Says me.

RORY: Ah, but your opinion has always been questionable at best.

GEMMA: You won't miss it then, will you.

She turns to leave. He makes a big show of gesturing to the wine.

RORY: This is good stuff. Argentinian.

GEMMA: So's Diego Maradona, and he's a massive handball cunt.

RORY: Gemma, do you kiss your mother with that mouth?

GEMMA: I kiss yours with it.

RORY: My mum's dead.

GEMMA: No wonder her breath's so bad.

Pause.

Sorry. I didn't mean to –

RORY: It's fine. Just a joke ain't it.

A silence.

GEMMA: So why am I here?

RORY: Most girls would give their right arm to be –

GEMMA: I'm leaving.

GEMMA *starts towards the door.*

RORY: Gem…

GEMMA *is at the door.*

I need to talk to you, okay.

GEMMA: About what?

RORY: About stuff.

GEMMA: Stuff?

RORY: Yeah.

Beat.

GEMMA: Turn the lights on.

RORY: Then everyone will know we're here.

GEMMA: Perhaps we should have met somewhere that didn't involve breaking into then.

RORY: Where's the fun in that?

GEMMA: Not getting arrested.

RORY: As if we're going to get arrested.

GEMMA: Turn the lights on then. Prove it.

Pause.

I hate the dark.

RORY: That's why I brought candles.

GEMMA: If they aren't lit then they aren't a lot of fucking good.

RORY: Give us your lighter then.

GEMMA: You bought candles without having a lighter?

RORY: I knew you'd have one.

GEMMA: That's your life. Right there. That sentence. Your whole fucking life.

She hands him a lighter. He starts to light some candles.

RORY: Better?

GEMMA: Yes.

RORY: You gonna tick me a fag then as a reward?

GEMMA: Ponce.

RORY: You love it.

She hands him a packet of cigarettes.

Silk Cut?

GEMMA: You wanna go without?

RORY: Like drinking Diet Coke, ain't it? Your teeth will still fall out, you'll just have a shit time while they do.

GEMMA: Lick the filter.

RORY: I know how to smoke a fag.

GEMMA: Then stop going on about it and smoke.

They both lick the filters. Light up.

RORY: Might as well smoke fresh air.

GEMMA: You wanted to talk. To do that it generally involves speaking actual words.

RORY: What have I been doing then?

GEMMA: Conjuring shite with your mouth. It's like going out with a magician.

RORY: Magicians are all phoneys. No such thing as magic.

GEMMA: Least they get paid.

RORY: I get paid.

GEMMA: The dole is not getting paid.

RORY: Money goes in my pocket. How else would you describe it?

GEMMA: Sponging.

RORY: That's not very socialist of you.

GEMMA: Neither is contributing nothing to society.

RORY: I'm not a socialist.

GEMMA: What are you then?

RORY: Thirsty.

He leans down and unscrews the cap off the wine.

GEMMA: Thought you said this was good wine?

RORY: It is.

GEMMA: Everyone knows screw caps are cheap shit.

RORY: *Au contrair, Gemma.* With modern corking techniques the screw cap is actually just as –

GEMMA: Learn that on a wine course, did you?

RORY: Fat Frank at the Offie.

GEMMA: That well-known wine connoisseur.

RORY: He works in a wine shop.

GEMMA: I work for a power plant. Doesn't mean I can make electricity, does it?

RORY: I dunno… You turn me on.

GEMMA *makes a gagging noise.*

Drink your fucking wine.

Pause.

GEMMA: We don't always have to get pissed.

RORY: What you want to do instead then?

He smiles at her, knowingly.

GEMMA: Yeah, you'll be lucky.

He slumps back. Takes a large glug of his wine.

As he puts down the glass **GEMMA** *grabs him and kisses him hard on the mouth.*

RORY: What was that for?

GEMMA: Coz I wanted to.

He goes to kiss her back. She puts up a hand stopping him.

But that doesn't mean that I want to again.

RORY: You tease.

GEMMA: Not yet anyway.

Pause.

Did you bring any cushions?

RORY: Yeah, I've got a rucksack full of fucking cushions. Stole them off the sofa before I left, didn't I?

GEMMA: Get piles sitting on the floor like this.

RORY: You're not supposed to talk about piles with your boyfriend.

GEMMA: Who said you were my boyfriend?

RORY: You did.

GEMMA: I did not.

RORY: Well, you implied.

GEMMA: Implied?

RORY: You… We… You know.

GEMMA: Is your dad waiting in the dark and this is actually a surprise wedding ceremony?

RORY: No, but –

GEMMA: We fucked, Rory. That doesn't mean I'm your girlfriend.

RORY: More than once.

GEMMA: Twice.

RORY: Three times.

GEMMA: The first time didn't count.

RORY: Yes it did.

GEMMA: Trust me. It didn't.

> *Beat.*

> I'm only winding you up. It was… Nice.

RORY: Nice?

GEMMA: Yeah.

RORY: Fucking hell.

GEMMA: Nice is alright.

RORY: Alright? Fucking hell, Gem.

GEMMA: Better than nice. Better than alright.

RORY: Great.

GEMMA: Not great. But not shit either.

> *Beat.*

RORY: Nice, eh?

GEMMA: Yeah, nice.

> *A moment.*

> Can we sit on the boat?

RORY: If you want. Wouldn't want you ruining your arsehole on my account.

GEMMA: You really should learn to keep your mouth shut.

RORY: Help me move the candles you stroppy cow.

> *They both stand and blow out the candles. The room is plunged into darkness.*

> *Moments pass.*

A noise.

The torch comes on. **GEMMA** *is in* **RORY**'s *arms.*

GEMMA: Did you hear that?

RORY: What?

GEMMA: That noise.

RORY: Probably just a rat.

GEMMA: Urgh.

> **RORY** *grabs hold of the lifeboat (it's a RIB, one of the inflatable ones rather than a huge full scale boat) and pulls himself up onto it.*

RORY: You'll be safe from them up here.

He offers his hand.

GEMMA: Yeah?

RORY: Can't promise about the crabs though.

GEMMA: Crabs!

Beat.

I thought you told me you'd been checked out.

RORY: Funny.

She passes him the candles and wine, which he takes and places on the boat.

He then offers his hand again and pulls her up onto the boat with him.

She shines the torch at his face without thinking.

RORY: Don't point that in my eyes.

He pushes her hand away, so it points in a different direction.

GEMMA: Light the candles then.

She holds the torch at his face again.

RORY: Okay, okay. Be careful though. This thing's worth a fucking packet.

GEMMA: It's an inflatable boat.

RORY: A very fucking expensive inflatable boat.

GEMMA: Yawn.

RORY: Us getting a new boat is a big deal.

GEMMA: *Us?*

RORY: The RNLI.

GEMMA: All anyone has talked about for the last fucking year.

RORY: It's a big deal.

> *Beat.*

GEMMA: I can lend them my Lilo if we break it.

RORY: Can your Lilo get to the middle of the estuary in a minute if there's an emergency?

GEMMA: Not with your fat arse on it.

> *She starts to light the candles. Carefully.*

You're always on eggshells when we're in here. Another reason why we should have gone to the pub.

RORY: You're not even drinking.

GEMMA: Don't have to drink at the pub.

RORY: What else you gonna do?

GEMMA: Play on the fruities. Pool. Darts. Have a dance.

RORY: Sounds shit.

GEMMA: Yeah, I definitely prefer sitting in a rat and crab infested Lifeboat station to that.

RORY: I wanted to see you.

> *She shines the torch on her face.*

GEMMA: Happy?

RORY: Yes.

The candles are all now lit.

From their light we can start to make out more of the RIB that they are sat on.

GEMMA *turns the torch off so now it's just the candles illuminating.*

GEMMA: Saw your dad on the way down here.

RORY: Gem… I wanted this to be romantic.

GEMMA: He was out the front with all the crew. Smashed all of them were. Be fucked if they have a call out tonight.

RORY: There's always a couple who would make the shout.

GEMMA: Not you though.

RORY: That meant to be funny?

Beat.

I jacked it in. My choice.

A silence.

It's a shit job anyway. Was just keeping that old prick happy. Only reason I went for it was to get him off my back.

GEMMA: So you're not going to try again?

RORY: No.

GEMMA: There's nothing to be embarrassed about.

RORY: I'm not fucking embarrassed.

GEMMA: Just do the test again.

RORY: Been driving boats since I was ten.

GEMMA: It's really not that big of a –

RORY: You the fucking expert now then?

Beat.

How do you know I failed the test?

GEMMA: I saw your dad. I said.

RORY: Why you speaking to him behind my back?

GEMMA: I'm not.

RORY: So you just *bumped into him* and he *just so happened* to tell you?

GEMMA: It's just a test. Everyone fails tests. I had to take my Maths O level five times. Who cares?

RORY: I'm asking you why you were talking to my dad?

GEMMA: And I'm telling you to take the test again.

RORY: You don't get it, do you?

GEMMA: All you've ever wanted is to be part of the crew. I've had to listen to you banging on about boats and wind and tides for the last ten years. You don't get to just bottle it now because you had a setback. That's fucking cowardly. You want this. I know you do.

RORY: You don't know me.

GEMMA: Who fucking does then, Rory? If I don't know you who does?

A silence.

Take the test again. It'll go better. I promise.

RORY: You can't promise that.

GEMMA: Yes, I c–

RORY: It was the eyesight test.

A silence.

You understand now?

Pause.

GEMMA: You can go to a doctor.

RORY: And he'll do what?

GEMMA: Make you better. That's what doctors do.

A moment.

RORY: It doesn't matter.

GEMMA: Course it does.

Pause.

I'm sorry. Really, I am.

RORY: Yeah me too.

A silence.

RORY *grabs a glass and starts to fill it back up with wine. He slugs it back in one.*

Pours another.

Have one.

GEMMA: A small one.

He pours her a glass. In no way is it small.

GEMMA *brings the glass to her lips. Takes the tiniest of sips.*

They told you this was good wine?

Beat.

I'm joking. It's lovely.

RORY: Should be at that price too.

GEMMA: But I'm worth it.

RORY: Yes. Yes, you are.

Pause.

GEMMA: You'll be okay. You'll find something else.

RORY: Yeah?

GEMMA: Yeah.

RORY: Such a town of opportunity ain't it, Mersea. Only time anyone has ever heard of it is when they think it's the river in fucking

Liverpool. Then they look disappointed when you tell them it's actually just a shitty little island in Essex.

GEMMA: Could be worse. Could be born in Ipswich.

He laughs. Happy to let a little bit of emotion out.

RORY: You aren't born in Ipswich, Gemma. You are pulled kicking and screaming from your dad's sister's womb.

GEMMA: Your mum was born in Ipswich.

RORY: She was also my aunt.

GEMMA: If she was here now she'd whip you black and blue.

RORY: That she would.

Beat.

GEMMA: Fucking hell, I was meant to be trying to cheer you up and I start going on about your mum.

RORY: I like talking about her.

GEMMA: Good.

RORY: Preferably not you kissing her though.

GEMMA: Noted.

Pause.

RORY: You could try and cheer me up in another way…

GEMMA: That why you've splashed out on this fancy wine? And candles.

RORY: Candles really aren't that expensive.

GEMMA: As if you bought them. They've got RNLI stamped all over –

RORY: I repurposed them.

GEMMA: Maybe I'm not in the mood.

RORY: That's not why I brought candles.

GEMMA: Is it so I can see about as well as you in this light, blind boy?

Beat.

Too soon?

RORY: Much too soon.

GEMMA: Got to laugh ain't you? Better than crying.

RORY: You see me crying?

GEMMA: I can't actually see fuck all because –

RORY: Do you know what day it is?

GEMMA: Friday. Next question.

RORY: The date?

GEMMA: Did you get me here to take part in the world's shittest pub quiz?

RORY: It's Halloween.

GEMMA: Yes. Having to dodge ten year olds throwing eggs on the way here was the giveaway.

RORY: So…

GEMMA: So?

RORY: So you like scary stuff.

GEMMA: No I don't.

RORY: You do. You told me.

GEMMA: When?

RORY: When we were in school together.

GEMMA: We were in school for eleven years. You are going to have to be a bit more specific.

RORY: In English. When you sat next to me.

GEMMA: First year?

RORY: Yeah.

GEMMA: You remembered that?

    Pause.

RORY: Yeah…

    Beat.

GEMMA: Do you love me?

RORY: Fuck off.

GEMMA: Have you always loved me?

RORY: Fuck. Off.

GEMMA: Awwwww, the blind boy loves me.

RORY: Gemma for fucksake.

GEMMA: I love you too.

    A moment.

RORY: Yeah?

GEMMA: Yeah.

    A silence.

RORY: I thought we could tell ghost stories. Tonight.

GEMMA: Are you ten?

RORY: It's Halloween.

GEMMA: Yeah, but you don't see me carving out a pumpkin either do you?

RORY: Well actually…

    He turns to his bag and starts to rummage through it.

    While he is distracted **GEMMA** *pours the remnants of her glass of wine away carefully trying to mask the sound.*

    RORY *eventually finds what he is looking for. A miniature pumpkin. Freshly carved.*

Impressed?

GEMMA: A little bit.

RORY: That took me hours.

GEMMA: You need to get a hobby.

RORY: I've got one. Pumpkin carving.

> **RORY** *takes a candle and places it in the pumpkin. Lights it.*

No torch after this. Just candles.

GEMMA: This seems a bit dumb.

> *He takes the torch and puts it under his chin lighting up his face.*

RORY: Are you scared?

GEMMA: No, of course I'm not scared.

RORY: If you're scared it's okay.

GEMMA: I'm not fucking scared.

> *There's a loud noise from somewhere in the room.* **GEMMA** *jumps.*

That doesn't fucking count.

> **RORY** *laughs.*

RORY: I'll go first.

GEMMA: You prepared one.

RORY: I didn't prepare one.

GEMMA: Aw, that's sweet.

RORY: Everyone knows a ghost story.

GEMMA: Have you learned it by heart?

RORY: You don't have to learn them by heart.

GEMMA: Well, go on then.

RORY: Drink first.

GEMMA: I'm fine.

RORY: Your glass is empty.

GEMMA: I have drank then, haven't I?

RORY: Drink more. Drink good.

He tops up her glass with more wine.

Helps with the ambience.

GEMMA: What the fuck do you know about ambience?

RORY: Fat Frank said –

GEMMA: Has Fat Frank turned into fucking Yoda since the last time I saw him?

RORY: He does have that green kind of tinge to him.

GEMMA: And hairy ears.

RORY: Never seen him hold a light sabre though.

GEMMA: You've never seen Fat Frank hold his light sabre? He always holds it out for me.

RORY: You dirty bitch.

GEMMA: You love it.

Beat.

RORY: He hasn't ever really shown you his –

GEMMA: No of course he fucking hasn't! Doubt he could even find it under that belly.

RORY: Good. For a minute there –

GEMMA: Tell your fucking story will you. Jesus.

RORY: Alright, alright.

Beat.

You promise not to cry if you get scared?

GEMMA: Do you want me to stay?

RORY: Yes.

GEMMA: Do you want me to potentially take some clothes off later this evening?

RORY: Yes.

GEMMA: Then don't keep saying that.

RORY: Okay.

He takes a breath.

So, there's this girl…

GEMMA: What's her name?

RORY: I don't know.

GEMMA: Great start.

RORY: Gemma.

GEMMA: She sounds hot.

RORY: She's not.

GEMMA *playfully slaps him.*

Watch the candles.

GEMMA: Get on with the story then!

RORY: So there's this girl –

GEMMA: Who is smoking hot.

RORY: She's at least a seven out of ten.

GEMMA: At least.

RORY: And she's trying to earn a little bit of extra cash by babysitting at some posh people's house in the nearby village.

GEMMA: Babysitters really get the shitty end of the stick, don't they?

RORY: What do you mean?

GEMMA: Always the babysitter ain't it? I already know that bad shit is going to happen to her.

RORY: Says who?

GEMMA: Says me you cretin. That's how these stories work.

RORY: Maybe this one's different.

GEMMA: I highly doubt that. What did all the babysitters do to get such a hard time of everything? Just look after everyone's kids so they can go out and get pissed. Hardly a crime is it?

RORY: Anyway…

GEMMA: Anyway.

RORY: So this nice girl goes round to the house and the mum says to her that the two kids are already asleep in bed, so really all she has to do is watch some TV and check on them every now and again to make sure everything's alright. Then they leave. And the girl is all alone in the house.

The phone rings… She answers it thinking it might be the nice parents, maybe they forgot to tell her something. You know. Some special thing she needs to do for their kids. But instead all she hears is…

Upstairs cutting up squares.

Hello?

Upstairs cutting up squares.

I don't know who this is?

Two chances left and then the theft.

The phone goes dead. And the girl is freaking out a bit and for a second she thinks about calling the parents. But she changes her mind. It's probably just kids messing about. So she turns the TV back on. Tries to relax. Forget about it.

The phone rings again.

GEMMA *holds her nose and does a mechanical kind of voice.*

GEMMA: Would you be interested in getting a conservatory fitted to your house?

RORY: Gemma for fucksake.

GEMMA: I'm sorry, I'm sorry.

RORY: This time the girl knows that something's up. But it's like those horror films. She just can't help but answer the phone. Even though she knows. Even though deep down she knows what's at the other end.

Upstairs cutting up squares.
One chance left then the theft.

She starts to shout

I'm going to ring the police if you call again.
I am.
I…

But the phone's already dead. And she starts to get this feeling of embarrassment. Embarrassment about how scared she is. So she turns up the television. And she just sits there. Alone. Terrified.

GEMMA: This isn't a ghost story.

RORY: It's a scary story.

GEMMA: I don't like it.

RORY: You want me to stop?

GEMMA: No, I'm just saying –

RORY: You scared?

GEMMA: No, I'm just saying –

RORY: The phone rings for the third time and now the babysitter is paralysed with fear. She knows. She knows it's not just kids playing a prank. That this is really one of those things that you think about in the middle of the night. One of those nightmares.

Upstairs cutting up squares

GEMMA: Rory

RORY: *No chances left*

GEMMA: Rory…

RORY: *Now the theft*

> And she's screaming this time.
> She's screaming down the phone
> LEAVE ME ALONE
> LEAVE ME ALONE
> And as she's dialling the police she thinks she hears a noise upstairs so she stands by the front door. And when the police answer and she tells them what's happening and they tell her to get out of the house immediately and not to go anywhere near the children's room. She realises that she hasn't thought for one second since the calls started to go and check on them.
> She realises that.
> And yet she still runs out the door and into the street.

> **GEMMA** *holds out her hand.*

GEMMA: Give me the torch

> **RORY** *puts it behind his back out of reach and continues.*

RORY: When the police arrive, they wrap a blanket around her and go into the house. They come out after ten minutes and say it's empty. That she should come back inside. And she can't stop herself… She can't stop herself from asking if the children are in there.

> The policeman's silence... That was enough of an answer.

GEMMA: Give. Me. The. Torch.

RORY: So they just sit there waiting for the parents to come back.
The ever so nice middleclass parents.
And when the mother came through the door…
The look on her face…
Horror.
Just horror.

And it was as they were sat there
In that fucking awkward silence

GEMMA *stand up on the boat.*

GEMMA: Fuck you, I'm going home.

GEMMA *goes to try and get down. But a noise comes from somewhere in the dark sending her falling back to where* **RORY** *is perched over the candles.*

RORY: The bag came crashing through the window. And even though the bag was stained and dirty, the mother couldn't help herself from walking towards it…

And opening it ever so slightly…

GEMMA: Shut up.

RORY: And that's when she saw them…
There in that bag…

GEMMA: Shut up, Rory.

RORY: Her babies…
Cut into tiny precise –

GEMMA: Shut up! Shut up shut up shut up shut up!!!!

A moment.

RORY: Bit of an overreaction.

GEMMA *is crying.*

Are you…

She turns her face away from him.

Gem….

GEMMA: Just leave me alone.

RORY: Gem, I was only trying to scare you a bit. You always said that you liked being –

GEMMA: You just don't get it, do you?

RORY: It was just a story.

GEMMA: You prick.

RORY: I thought –

GEMMA: No, that's one thing you didn't do. The one thing you never fucking do. Just because you fucked up your life doesn't mean you have to fuck up everyone else's.

RORY: How have I fucked up your life?

Pause.

Gemma?

A silence.

GEMMA: It doesn't matter. Go again.

RORY: What do you mean *'go again'*.

GEMMA: Tell me another story.

RORY: What's the matter with you?

GEMMA: Nothing. Go again.

RORY: I don't want to go again. I want you to tell me –

GEMMA: Well I don't know any shit ghost stories, so why else are we here?

A moment.

RORY: I'm leaving.

GEMMA: Thank fuck for that. Let's go to the pub.

RORY: Mersea. Tonight.

A long silence.

Come with me.

GEMMA: What?

RORY: Fuck this place. Come with me.

Beat.

GEMMA: Where are we going to go?

RORY: London.

GEMMA: Who do you know in London?

RORY: People.

GEMMA: What people?

RORY: One of Frank's mates said we can crash with him for a bit.

GEMMA: Fat Frank?

RORY: Yes.

GEMMA: So the bloke from the Offie is now an estate agent as well?

RORY: What does it matter if we get out of here.

GEMMA: We don't know anyone there.

RORY: I just said –

GEMMA: The fat bloke from the Offie's mate doesn't fucking count Rory!

RORY: We'll make friends. New friends. Go to bars and clubs and do stuff. Actual fucking stuff.

GEMMA: And how are we going to pay for that stuff?

RORY: I've got money.

GEMMA: Pretty sure the dole money ain't going to –

He pulls his bag forward and unzips it. Takes out a wedge of cash.

Where did you get that?

RORY: It's not important. You said we need money, I've got money.

GEMMA: Tell me where you got it from?

A silence.

You robbed it didn't you?

RORY: And what?

GEMMA: You fucking idiot.

RORY: We need it more than they do.

GEMMA: This is about the test isn't it. You get turned down for the RNLI and in the same week you just decide to –

She laughs a wry laugh. To herself.

It's from the fundraiser, isn't it?

RORY: No.

GEMMA: Don't fucking lie to me.

RORY: Stop asking me so many questions then. Just say yes.

GEMMA: You stole money from a charity.

RORY: It's not a charity.

GEMMA: What is it then?

RORY: Got their new boat already haven't they. What does it matter?

GEMMA: So that makes it alright then?

RORY: I'm not saying that.

GEMMA: You need to put it back before your dad notices.

RORY: I don't care if he notices. I want him to notice.

Pause.

You know what he said to me? When I told him about the test?

'*Not surprised.*' Not fucking surprised.

GEMMA: He was probably just disappointed too.

RORY: Sounded like it.

GEMMA: Running away won't help.

RORY: We're seventeen, Gem. It's not running away. It's growing up. Leaving this poxy little island. That's all. We're one hour away from

London by train but it feels like it's on the other side of a the planet. The fucking universe. Don't you want to just get out of here?

GEMMA: It won't magically make everything better.

RORY: Maybe it will.

Pause..

GEMMA: What do I tell my mum?

RORY: Don't tell her anything.

GEMMA: Who's going to look after her?

RORY: Your sister.

GEMMA: Along with her kids and her layabout husband? Well, she is going to love that.

RORY: I don't care about anyone else. Just us.

Beat.

Don't be angry with me.

GEMMA: Why not?

RORY: I'm doing this for us.

GEMMA: Your old man will call the police. He's not stupid.

RORY: He won't. He'll be too ashamed to do that.

Pause.

I'll make the money back. Donate it to the RNLI in London.

GEMMA: Everyone would know.

RORY: Fuck them. We'll never see them again.

GEMMA: You don't think anyone from round here ever goes to London?

RORY: No. Not really. Do you?

Beat.

Work on the boats or work in the power plant or if you're really lucky then get a job on the fucking caravan site in East Mersea. Like a riptide this place. Fight against it you just get pulled further down.

A silence.

GEMMA: So we just run off and no one ever hears from us again?

RORY: Exactly. I'd look after you. You know that.

GEMMA: You can barely look after yourself.

RORY: I like you more than I like myself.

A silence.

GEMMA: I can't.

RORY: Yes. You can.

GEMMA: I… I just…

RORY: What?

She shakes her head.

GEMMA: Nothing.

A silence.

RORY: You didn't even consider it.

GEMMA: I did.

RORY: No, you didn't. You thought I was joking. Just like everyone else always does. Big fucking joke, ain't it? Me. My life. Ho-fucking-ho.

GEMMA: I don't think that.

RORY: But you still won't come will you?

GEMMA: No.

Pause.

You bring me out here and tell me a shitty story about kids getting killed then ask me to run off to London with you. Does that sound sane to you Rory? Does that sound like a good fucking deal? What did you expect?

Silence.

RORY: Not much else to say then is there.

He blows the candle out in the pumpkin. Turns the torch on. Starts to pack up the wine and glasses.

GEMMA: Rory…

RORY: It's fine.

GEMMA: This isn't about how I feel about you.

RORY: You don't have to make excuses.

GEMMA: I'm not.

RORY: Yes. You are.

He grabs his rucksack and puts it on his back. Hops down from the boat to the floor.

GEMMA: Why does everything have to be all or fucking nothing with you?

RORY: Because that's the only way you know if anything matters.

GEMMA: You're really just going to leave me here?

RORY: Why would I stay?

He hands her the torch.

Have a nice life, Gem.

GEMMA: Rory…

He moves into the dark of the station. We can now only hear him rather than see him.

You selfish prick.

A metal door clangs. Then a short burst of light crashes into the room as **RORY** *exits. We see* **GEMMA***'s face awash with tears in this brief moment.*

What if I had something to tell you as well, hey?

The door shuts sending the room back to black.

2.

West Mersea Caravan Park. The beach. Seventeen years later. Winter.

A huge moon illuminates the coastline. In the distance we can see the wind farm in the estuary. Bradwell power station. Some old derelict boats.

RORY, *now thirty-four, stands at the front of the shore.*

He skims a stone.

Skims another one.

Starts to search around for some more.

Skims another one.

Another.

He sits.

Takes out a cigarette. Starts to smoke.

Produces a bottle from a bag next to him. Drinks.

ISLA, *seventeen, enters. She stands for a time watching* **RORY**.

ISLA: They have a name for people like you.

RORY: Fucking cool?

ISLA: Not quite sure it goes like that.

    ISLA *walks over to him.*

RORY: You're late.

ISLA: You're early.

RORY: I <u>was</u> early.

ISLA: Sorry.

RORY: If you do the same thing every time we meet, it probably negates the apology.

ISLA: *Negates?* Oooo, posh.

RORY: You were the one who wanted to swap nights.

ISLA: I have a social life, dad. Shoot me.

RORY: Could have at least turned up on time.

ISLA: Wanna moan about it all night?

RORY: I'm not moaning.

ISLA: Sounds like it.

RORY: You haven't been the one stood out here in the cold on your own like a prick for an hour.

ISLA: Looks like you found some company.

She reaches for the bottle. He moves it away from her.

RORY: You're seventeen.

ISLA: You remembered. Well done.

RORY: I've never forgotten one of your birthdays.

ISLA: Missed a few though.

Beat.

Gimme a sip.

RORY: It's rum. You won't like it.

ISLA: I know what rum tastes like.

RORY: Neat. Rum.

ISLA: We just call that a shot nowadays, Dad.

He hands her the bottle.

RORY: A small sip. That's all. And don't tell your mother.

ISLA: That was the first thing I was going to do when I get home. So I'll cross it off the itinerary.

RORY: You're too smart for someone your age.

ISLA: You're too dumb.

She takes the bottle and necks a large gulp.

Retches.

RORY: There we go.

ISLA: What the fuck is that?!

RORY: Watch your language.

ISLA: Seriously. That is not rum.

RORY: Yes. It is.

ISLA: Rum tastes like coconuts.

>   **RORY** *sighs.*

>   It does.

RORY: That's called Bacardi.

>   *Pause.*

ISLA: Can I have another sip?

RORY: You just nearly puked.

ISLA: Coz you didn't tell me you were drinking methylated spirits.

RORY: Thought you were used to shots.

ISLA: I am.

RORY: See how that sits. You hold it down you can have another in five minutes.

ISLA: Boring.

RORY: You'll thank me later.

>   *Pause.*

ISLA: Sorry I was late.

RORY: It's fine.

ISLA: Some bellend tried to drive across The Strood at high tide.

RORY: Lifeboat out?

ISLA: Yeah, fucked traffic for about an hour.

RORY: You'd think people would learn you can't take a Fiesta across a road filled with water wouldn't you?

ISLA: Go fast enough you can.

RORY: Bet he thought that too.

ISLA: Maybe they should just raise the fucking road. Not hard is it. The tide comes up to here. Let's make the one road on and off the island higher than it.

Beat.

RORY: At least you got to spend some more time on the bus. You do love that bus journey home.

ISLA: Funny.

RORY: Probably a tourist.

ISLA: Car looked new.

RORY: Definitely a tourist then. The dickheads.

ISLA: You ain't moaning when you're serving them breakfast.

RORY: No, but they are! Avocados with eggs? Who wants something fucking green for breakfast? If they want that they can fuck off over to Coggeshall.

ISLA: I went to school in Coggeshall.

RORY: But you never turned into one of those pretentious twats.

ISLA: Still time yet.

RORY: Nah, you've got enough of me in you.

ISLA: Well that's a shit compliment if I've ever heard one.

Beat.

How is it? The job?

RORY: It's cooking breakfasts for fat wankers staying here because they couldn't afford Clacton.

ISLA: It's work.

RORY: Yeah.

ISLA: Good for you. Gives you something to do.

RORY: I can think of better things.

ISLA: And those are things that get you into trouble.

RORY: That weren't my fault.

ISLA: He needed stitches, Dad.

RORY: How do you know?

ISLA: I live here. I know everyone that lives here. So if you smash some bloke up down the Victory, chances are I know.

RORY: You wanna find better mates then.

ISLA: People talk. You know that.

RORY: Don't mean you have to listen.

ISLA: I –

RORY: Wanna mind your own business or you'll end up like the rest of them on this godforsaken island.

ISLA: You're my dad.

RORY: I am.

ISLA: Then it is my business, isn't it?

Pause.

RORY: Should have kept his mouth shut. Then he wouldn't have been picking up his teeth at the end of the night then.

A silence.

ISLA: Wasn't good for you anyway. Being in a pub all the time.

RORY: I'm a grown man, Isla.

ISLA: I know that.

RORY: Don't take the piss then.

ISLA: I'm not

RORY: I don't need my daughter telling me what's good for me.

> **RORY** *stands up, picks a stone and skims it out to sea.*

ISLA: Five? You're losing your touch.

RORY: Practice go.

ISLA: You not get some of that in while you were waiting on me?

RORY: Was practising my other hobby.

> *He lifts the bottle.*

ISLA: That's neither big nor clever.

RORY: You won't want any more then?

ISLA: I meant drinking alone.

RORY: I'm not alone now, am I?

> *Pause.*

ISLA: We just going to stand here and skim stones then?

RORY: You like skimming stones.

ISLA: I liked skimming stones when I was ten. Thought this was meant to be *quality father daughter time.*

RORY: It is.

> **RORY** *picks up a stone and gives it to* **ISLA**. *She skims it out across the water.*
>
> A three?

ISLA: Shit stone. Your fault.

RORY: Oh, yeah, would be my fault wouldn't it?

ISLA: It wasn't even flat.

RORY: Poor workman blames his tools.

ISLA: Her.

RORY: What?

ISLA: Blames <u>her</u> tools. Sexism isn't cool anymore, Dad.

RORY: Next you'll be saying that smoking isn't either.

He holds up a packet of fags.

She reaches for one. He pulls it back.

ISLA: I won't tell Mum.

RORY: Good girl.

She takes a cigarette.

ISLA: Lighter?

He searches his pockets.

RORY: I'm sure I had one on me.

ISLA *takes out a lighter.*

ISLA: Here.

RORY: Ta.

He lights both of their cigarettes.

ISLA: She's given up.

RORY: Your mother?

ISLA: Yeah.

He laughs. Bitter.

RORY: Figures.

ISLA: How?

RORY: She was the first person who gave me a fag. If I get cancer that'll be her fault too.

ISLA: Can we not.

He knows. Moves on.

RORY: You still seeing that boy?

ISLA: Fuck off, Dad.

RORY: You liked him didn't you?

ISLA: That was ages ago.

RORY: It was last time I saw you.

ISLA: Yeah.

> *Beat.*

> Let's get back to skimming stones, hey?

> **ISLA** *looks around for a stone.*

> Here we go.

> *She brings it back to him. It's virtually a boulder.*

RORY: With that?

ISLA: Least it's flat. Unlike the one you got me.

RORY: Give it here.

> *She passes him the rock.*

> *He throws it out across the water.*

> *Throws his hands up triumphantly.*

ISLA: How the fuck did you do that?

RORY: Technique.

ISLA: Still didn't break the record.

RORY: With that? Are you joking.

ISLA: I don't believe you ever got a ten.

RORY: You were here.

ISLA: I don't remember.

RORY: Not my fault you've got a shit memory.

ISLA: Genetically, it probably is.

RORY: If you got me the right stone I could do it again.

ISLA: Dad… I need to ask you something.

RORY: I'm not buying you booze again.

ISLA: I need to borrow some money.

RORY: I thought you had a job.

ISLA: I have got a job.

RORY: Well then.

ISLA: It's not enough.

RORY: Enough for what?

ISLA: Me and Danielle are going to –

RORY: Danielle Church? I thought I told you not to hang around with her.

ISLA: And I thought I told you you're not in charge of my life.

RORY: I'm serious.

ISLA: So am I.

RORY: I know her family.

ISLA: So do I.

RORY: Her brother. Daniel…

ISLA: Yes.

RORY: You have to ask questions about a family that call their two kids Daniel and Danielle.

ISLA: It's funny.

RORY: Your kid's names ain't meant to be funny.

ISLA: We've found a place. It's not big. Just a room really. In Chelmsford.

A silence.

You gonna say something or what?

RORY: You ain't moving to Chelmsford.

ISLA: Yes. I am.

RORY: You're seventeen.

ISLA: Nearly eighteen.

RORY: And what about your job?

ISLA: They've got an office there. They said if it goes well they could look at me moving to the London one –

RORY: It ain't happening.

ISLA: Dad.

RORY: We didn't agree to this.

ISLA: *We?*

RORY: Your mum and me.

ISLA: You and Mum haven't said more than hello to each other since the day I was born.

RORY: I know your mother.

ISLA: You really don't.

Pause.

RORY: We agreed on you leaving college. We agreed that you'd stay here. On the island.

ISLA: I don't need your permission.

RORY: You need my money though.

Beat.

ISLA: I thought you'd be pleased.

RORY: That my daughter wants to fuck off to that poncy commuter town full of wankers? Yeah, I'm over the moon.

ISLA: That I was getting out.

RORY: And why would that make me happy?

ISLA: You hate it here.

RORY: No I don't. I hate the people.

    ISLA *laughs.*

ISLA: The people who live in a place are a place, Dad.

RORY: Shame all the cunts ended up here.

ISLA: I live here.

RORY: Not for long it would seem.

ISLA: Mum lives here.

RORY: You making my point for me?

ISLA: Don't say that.

RORY: I was joking.

ISLA: It wasn't funny.

    Pause.

RORY: Look.

ISLA: What am I looking at?

RORY: The sea.

ISLA: It's an estuary.

RORY: Don't be smart.

ISLA: I'm not.

RORY: It's beautiful. You take all the people on this island and fuck them off, it would be the best place on god's green earth.

    Pause.

    What does your mum think?

ISLA: When have you ever cared about what –

RORY: Just tell me what she thinks, Isla.

ISLA: She's fine with it. Just can't help me out with the money.

RORY: Don't lie to me.

ISLA: I'm not.

RORY: I'll call her.

ISLA: No. You won't.

RORY: I will. You want to try me?

>   **ISLA** *takes out her phone. Holds it out to* **RORY**.

ISLA: Go on then.

>   *For a moment it looks like he might take it.*
>
>   *But he can't.*
>
>   *He takes a huge slug of rum from the bottle. Sits.*

ISLA: It's Chelmsford. It's hardly the other side of the planet. I'll still see you. And it's only the deposit. I can cover the rent.

>   *Pause.*

I wouldn't ask if I wasn't –

RORY: Your mum honestly said she was okay with this?

ISLA: Yeah.

>   *He laughs.*

What's funny?

RORY: My life. It's a fucking punchline.

ISLA: It's a really nice flat.

RORY: I stayed here for you. When I came back. You were the only reason I stayed.

ISLA: I didn't ask you to.

RORY: I ain't saying that.

ISLA: It's not my fault you're here.

RORY: I ain't saying that either.

ISLA: Can't you be proud of me?

RORY: I am.

Beat.

I don't have the money.

ISLA: You do. I know you do. When Nan died she left you loads.

RORY: What your nan left me is none of your business.

ISLA: Mum said you never touched it. Squirreled it away.

RORY: None of her business either.

ISLA: So it's gone then is it?

RORY: Yeah.

ISLA: What you spent it on then?

He lifts the bottle.

You don't drink that much.

RORY: You don't see me that much. Took a month to organise tonight.

ISLA: And what would we do if I did?

RORY: This. Spend time together.

ISLA: Yeah, real quality time ain't it.

RORY: You've never wanted for nothing.

ISLA: Coz Mum worked two jobs and never spent a penny on herself.

RORY: I helped.

ISLA: Yeah.

RORY: I offered.

ISLA: Yeah.

RORY: I did. Weren't my fault she wouldn't take anything.

ISLA: Course not. Nothing was your fault was it.

RORY: I didn't chose this.

ISLA: Who did then? Who made you steal that money? Who made you go to prison?

RORY: I was the exact same age as you are now when they sent me down. A child. He didn't have to prosecute. He didn't have to tell everyone on this whole fucking island that it was his son.

ISLA: You broke his heart.

RORY: Yeah, well he broke mine first.

Pause.

Didn't even make it off the island before the police picked me up. Spent my whole life trying to leave this fucking place and when I do it's in the back of a pig car. Locked up.

Beat.

First time I've ever woken up and not been able to hear the sea. You think things like that don't matter, but they do. The things you miss. The important things

ISLA: I'm going to Chelmsford not fucking prison, Dad.

RORY: You don't understand, Isla.

ISLA: Seems pretty fucking clear to me.

RORY: She never told me about you.

A silence.

I could handle the lack of visits. The fact that everyone just left me to fucking rot in that jail cell. But who keeps the fact a man has a child from him?

Beat.

Turned up here to collect my stuff after I got out. One last look at this shitty island and I'm gone. Then I see your mother and you walking down the street… And I know. I just know.

Pause.

ISLA: And you stayed.

RORY: Of course I stayed. You're my daughter. My blood.

Beat.

That place… The way people look at you after. Nobody ever forgets. Not round here.

Pause.

ISLA: Maybe you should have just left then.

RORY: Maybe I should.

Beat.

ISLA: I don't know why I bother.

She turns and starts to storm off.

RORY: Wait.

She's almost gone.

I'll give you the money.

She stops.

ISLA: Really?

RORY: Yeah. If it's what you want.

ISLA: You promise?

He nods.

She rushes over to him and hugs him.

RORY: But only if your mother agrees.

ISLA: She will. She has.

They sit.

Calls for a celebration…

He passes her the bottle.

She takes a big glug. Retches again.

Why would anyone choose to drink this?

RORY: You are, right now.

ISLA: If I could get served myself then I wouldn't be drinking this shit.

RORY: Bacardi Breezer, eh?

ISLA: No.

RORY: The idea of alcohol is that you can taste it.

ISLA: The idea of alcohol is to get pissed.

RORY: Pass me the fucking bottle then.

She passes him the bottle. He takes a large gulp.

You cold?

ISLA: A little.

He takes off his coat and wraps it round her.

ISLA: Thank you.

Pause.

RORY: Sorry about that. You know, before.

ISLA: You were just angry. That's all.

RORY: That's not an excuse.

ISLA: I stormed off.

RORY: You did. Maybe it runs in the family. The anger.

ISLA: Like father like daughter.

RORY: Your mother could go when she wanted to as well. She doesn't get off scot-free from this.

ISLA: Not like us.

RORY: I like that. That we share something.

ISLA: Course we do. I'm your daughter.

Pause.

RORY: She still seeing that fella?

ISLA: Is that any of your business?

RORY: I can still ask after her.

ISLA: If it matters that much ask her yourself.

RORY: And when would I do that?

ISLA: You live on an island the size of a postage stamp. It's not like you don't see each other.

Beat.

She isn't.

RORY: No?

ISLA: Haven't seen him round the house for ages.

RORY: Obviously not the one.

ISLA: Obviously.

RORY: You liked him didn't you?

ISLA: I didn't care either way.

RORY: She deserves someone. You know. To grow old with.

ISLA: She's old already. You both are.

RORY: Nice.

Beat.

Tell her I asked after her.

ISLA: Tell her yourself.

RORY: Isla…

ISLA: Dad.

RORY: Just do it will you.

ISLA: And then what?

>*Beat.*

>Maybe if you bothered to actually talk to each other, you might be able to sort everything out.

RORY: We do talk to each other.

ISLA: Through me.

RORY: Isla, if it's that big of a deal don't tell her.

ISLA: I don't mean now. I mean always. Since I can remember.

>*Pause.*

RORY: It never stopped either of us loving you.

ISLA: I didn't say it did.

RORY: When you grow up you'll understand.

ISLA: That's such bullshit.

RORY: You will.

ISLA: What if I want to understand now? What then? What if this is my last fucking day on the planet?

>*She puts her hand to her face. Turns sharply.* **RORY** *notices.*

RORY: Are you okay?

>*She's crying but desperately trying to hold it in.*

ISLA: You're both cowards.

RORY: Life is complicated, Isla.

ISLA: You both need to just get over yourselves. You ever thought about how much of a pain in the arse it is having to pass on your messages. Listen to you both bang on about each other –

RORY: She talks about me?

ISLA: Yeah, and?

Pause.

RORY: Really?

ISLA: Tells me not to ask you for any booze money.

RORY: Cut out the middleman tonight, didn't we?

Beat.

If your mum wanted to talk to me, she would have by now.

ISLA: That's such a cop out.

RORY: She doesn't deserve any grief from me.

ISLA: So now you can both be unhappy forever then?

RORY: Lot of people that are.

A silence.

ISLA: Wanna go up to your caravan? We could watch a film or something. Before I go out. I could show you the pictures of the place. Properly.

RORY: Rot your mind watching as much TV as you do.

ISLA: Sitting here will give you piles.

RORY *laughs heartedly.*

What, it will.

He laughs again.

What?

RORY: Nothing.

ISLA: If you don't look after your arse Dad, you can't expect anyone else to.

RORY: What kind thing is that to say?

ISLA: Just saying, it's hardly going to be a long time is it?

RORY: What isn't?

ISLA: When you're all old and that and in a home.

RORY: I'm thirty-four, Isla.

ISLA: Who will be wiping your arse then, hey? Won't be me, I'm telling you that.

RORY: Won't have any booze to bribe you with then.

ISLA: I'll get the carers to do it instead. I'm nice like that.

RORY: All heart ain't you.

> **ISLA** *picks up a stone and skims it out to sea.*

Five.

ISLA: I wasn't even trying.

RORY: You never do.

> *A moment.*

My old man used to bring me down here. This exact part of the beach. Used to scare the shit out of me. Tell all these scary stories of things that lived in the sea that would kidnap children. Lure them into the water to their –

ISLA: Life really must have been shit without the internet.

> **ISLA**'s *mobile phone starts to ring. She answers it straight away segueing straight into conversation with whoever is on the other end.*

Yesssssssss, mate. Where you at?

> *Pause.*

Uh-huh.

> *Pause.*

Uh-huh.

Pause.

Yeah.

Pause.

Yeah!

RORY: Do you have to –

ISLA: No, I'm still with him.

RORY: Isla…

ISLA: Nah, I won't be long.

She hangs up her phone and pockets it.

RORY: I wish you wouldn't do that.

ISLA: Excuse me for having friends.

RORY: You could have called her back.

ISLA: What if it was urgent?

RORY: Was it urgent?

ISLA: She was telling me where we're going out tonight.

RORY: So, no.

ISLA: So, one hundred percent yes.

RORY: I thought we were going to watch a film?

ISLA: You didn't say yes.

RORY: I didn't say no either.

ISLA: Well, this is a moment to moment thing, Dad. And your moment is now gone sadly.

RORY: What time are you leaving?

ISLA: She wants me to be there by –

RORY: Was it Danielle Church?

ISLA: Don't make this into a thing again. She's going to be my house mate.

RORY: I'm just saying I know her family. I know what they're like.

ISLA: Stop being such a dick.

RORY: I'm not being a dick, I'm just saying –

ISLA: Well don't.

RORY: Stay. We'll have a laugh. I promise.

ISLA: What's so wrong with them?

RORY: I'm not saying me and your mum are perfect, but –

ISLA: A mild understatement.

RORY: But we're good people. Deep down.

ISLA: In your opinion.

RORY: I never let fourteen year olds smoke pot in my house.

ISLA: Pot?

RORY: Yeah.

    ISLA *starts laughing loudly.*

ISLA: It's basically legal now, Dad.

RORY: Not when you're fourteen.

ISLA: I didn't go there when I was fourteen.

RORY: I know them. People don't change, Isla.

ISLA: That's a sad way to look at the world.

RORY: I've seen more of it than you.

ISLA: No, you haven't.

    Pause.

Will you give me a lift to meet her?

RORY *lifts the bottle of rum up.*

I'll be late otherwise.

RORY: She's your best mate, yeah?

ISLA: Yeah.

RORY: Then she already knows you're going to be late. You're always late.

Beat.

I'm over the limit.

ISLA: Everyone does it. It's hardly far is it.

RORY: I'm <u>over the limit</u>.

ISLA: It's only five minutes down the road.

RORY: Then walk.

ISLA: Okay, so it's not five minutes down the road.

RORY: Exactly.

ISLA: I just want to spend a bit more time with you.

Beat.

And I didn't bring out any money as I thought you were going to –

RORY: I'll lend you the bus fare.

ISLA: You really think I'm going to get a bus?

RORY: Too good for buses are we now?

ISLA: Yes. One hundred percent, yes.

Beat.

What's the point in having an ex-con as a father if he won't break the law for you?

RORY: A constant disappointment.

ISLA: You really are.

RORY *delves in his pocket takes out some coins.*

RORY: Here.

ISLA: Thanks Dad.

RORY: I'll sort out the money for that flat this week. Let me know where you want it transferred.

Beat.

And don't be coming in at all hours waking your mum up.

ISLA: I won't.

RORY: And don't be hanging around with that girl's brother.

ISLA: I won't Dad.

RORY: And don't you be having any fun whatsoever.

ISLA: Dad.

RORY: I love you.

ISLA: Dad!

RORY: I do.

ISLA *pulls him into a huge hug.*

ISLA: One last go? See if I can beat your record?

RORY: It ain't happening.

She looks around for a rock. Finds the one.

ISLA: This is the one.

RORY: Heard that before.

ISLA *walks to the front and skims the stone out.*

Eight.

ISLA: Nine.

RORY: Liar.

ISLA: You're just going blind in your old age.

She turns and starts to walk off.

RORY: Have a good night.

ISLA: I will.

She stops just before exiting.

I love you Dad.

Then she's gone.

RORY *takes a drink.*

Picks up a stone. Skims it out to sea.

His face lights up.

RORY: Isla!

He starts off after her.

And he's gone.

We stay with just the sea as it rolls in for a moment.

Then black.

3.

The Strood. Mersea Island. Late afternoon. Early Spring.

GEMMA, *now fifty-one, is stood next to a small collection of flowers on The Strood – the one road on and off Mersea Island to the mainland.*

She puts down some fresh flowers. Tidies some old ones that are now dead into a bag.

She takes out her purse and uses a wet wipe to clean a small name plaque.

Kneels. Prays.

Moments pass.

She takes out a cigarette. Goes to light it. The flint springs out of her lighter.

GEMMA: Fuck.

> *She tries the lighter again. It's clearly broken.*

> Serves you right you stupid old cow.

> **RORY**, *also now fifty-one, enters. He sees* **GEMMA**, *freezes in a weird kind of stasis.*

> I know you're there.

RORY: Yeah?

GEMMA: Yeah.

> *Pause.*

RORY: You want me to go?

GEMMA: You got somewhere to be?

RORY: Not so much.

GEMMA: Then who am I to tell you what to do.

> *Beat.*

RORY: I really can come back another –

GEMMA: Have you got a lighter?

> *He puts his hands in his pocket. Searches desperately. Fails.*

> Course not.

RORY: Some things don't change, hey?

GEMMA: Some do.

A silence.

RORY: It looks nice.

GEMMA: Good.

RORY: I always know when you've been.

GEMMA: Cigarette butts the giveaway?

RORY: Meant to take them with you now. Will have the council on you.

GEMMA: Oh yeah?

RORY: Fines and everything.

GEMMA: Still can't collect the bins on time though.

RORY: Modern life.

GEMMA: Yeah.

RORY puts his hand to his chest. The pocket in his shirt. Produces a lighter.

A miracle.

He passes it to her.

RORY: Knew I had it somewhere.

She lights her cigarette. Offers the box to RORY.

Just had one.

GEMMA: Ah, but they're fucking lovely, aren't they?

RORY: They are.

GEMMA: Have another one then. With me.

She passes him a cigarette. Lights it for him. She puts the lighter in her pocket.

See. Gorgeous. They can keep fucking about with the packets. They can hide them behind a safe in the corner shop. I'll still be having twenty Bensons and Hedges on a daily basis till they cart me off to the cemetery.

RORY: I thought you gave up?

GEMMA: Who has been spreading these vicious rumours about me?

RORY: It was…

Beat.

You know.

GEMMA: Oh…

Pause.

A brief moment of madness a long time ago. I have corrected the error of my ways.

RORY: Glad to hear it.

A silence.

GEMMA: You can say her name.

RORY: I know.

GEMMA: You stopped.

RORY: I know I did.

GEMMA: I just thought I should say.

Pause.

RORY: You don't own that. You don't get to own that.

GEMMA: I didn't say I did.

RORY: Telling me what I can and can't say. She was my daughter too.

GEMMA: What's your fucking problem?

Beat.

RORY: You know what… You stay. I'll come back another time.

He turns to exit.

GEMMA: Stop.

Pause.

Please. I didn't mean that. Honest.

He stops.

RORY: I didn't mean to bite.

GEMMA: You didn't. It was me.

RORY: Been working on it.

GEMMA: What?

RORY: Anger. Don't want to be that person anymore.

GEMMA: Reformed man, hey?

RORY: Who wants to be around an angry prick always flying off the handle.

GEMMA: You weren't that bad.

RORY: You missed the worst of it.

GEMMA: Suppose you had a few things to be angry about.

RORY: Maybe.

GEMMA: Suppose we both did.

A silence

GEMMA: The Lifeboat was just out.

RORY: Oh yeah? Someone misjudge the tide?

GEMMA: Just some jet ski wankers.

RORY: This time of year? They need their brains looking at.

GEMMA: Jet ski looked in better nick than the lifeboat.

RORY: They'll have the new one soon.

GEMMA: Fundraising going well?

Beat.

RORY: How would I know?

GEMMA: I hear you've been out shaking buckets.

RORY: Word travels fast.

GEMMA: Nothing stays a secret on this island long.

Beat.

It's good. That you're involved.

RORY: I was just shaking a bucket.

GEMMA: Even so.

A moment.

RORY: I thought you usually come in the morning. You know. On the day. I try and leave that for you.

GEMMA: That's kind. You don't need to.

RORY: All the same. Thought you might like some time alone. You know.

GEMMA: Have enough time on my own.

A silence.

Seventeen years. Not much of a life is it.

RORY: No.

GEMMA: Been saying to myself that I need to stop. That it doesn't help. You know. Coming here. But I just can't think of her being on her own on her birthday.

RORY: She's not on her own now is she.

Beat.

GEMMA: Can I borrow your lighter again?

RORY: You just put one out.

GEMMA: You keeping count?

RORY: No.

GEMMA: Good. Lighter please.

RORY: You actually pocketed it the last time.

GEMMA: I did not.

RORY: Seriously.

GEMMA: What an old lush.

RORY: You're not old.

GEMMA: I'm as old as you.

RORY: You look better for it.

GEMMA: Thank you.

She touches her pockets. Retrieves the lighter.

You should have said something.

RORY: It's just a lighter.

GEMMA: It's your lighter.

RORY: It's fine.

She lights another cigarette. Offers him his lighter back.

Seriously. Keep it.

GEMMA: I will.

He takes out a card.

RORY: Do you mind?

GEMMA: Of course not.

Beat.

I should be getting home anyway.

RORY: Stay.

GEMMA: Yeah?

RORY: Yeah.

Pause.

GEMMA: Okay.

RORY *moves to the side and places a card next to the flowers.* **GEMMA** *comes to next to him.*

You need to put them up here. Or the tide gets them.

RORY *laughs to himself.*

RORY: Really?

GEMMA: Yeah.

RORY: You mean every single thing I left here…

GEMMA: Yep.

RORY: Fucking hell.

GEMMA: I was going to come and knock. Tell you.

RORY: Was you?

GEMMA: No.

A shared smile.

RORY: That's a hell of a lot of money in cards.

GEMMA: She'd be wetting herself.

RORY: She always knew I was a cluster fuck.

GEMMA: You should know better. Being a man of the sea.

RORY: Hardly.

GEMMA: Runs in your blood.

RORY: Not anymore.

GEMMA: You want a tack? To pin it up with. I've got a load with me if –

RORY: You know what, I reckon I'll leave it.

GEMMA: Yeah?

RORY: I reckon she'd like that.

GEMMA: Better not let the council see you. If they are giving out fines for cigarettes, they'll cut your hands off for a whole card.

RORY: You can talk with all your flowers.

GEMMA: Biodegradable.

RORY: *Biodegradable*, eh? Fancy.

GEMMA: I'm an educated woman now.

RORY: Oh yeah?

GEMMA: Evening classes.

RORY: Check you.

GEMMA: The grief counsellor. She suggested it.

RORY: Oh.

GEMMA: Was just for something to do at the start. But now –

RORY: Enjoy it?

GEMMA: Yeah.

RORY: See you on *University Challenge* soon.

GEMMA: You watch *University Challenge*?

RORY: No.

GEMMA: Didn't think so.

RORY: Still know what it is though. Didn't have to go to a class for that.

Beat.

I've seen you in Tesco's.

GEMMA: I shop. Shouldn't be a surprise.

RORY: In the booze section.

GEMMA: I drink. I deserve a drink.

Beat.

RORY: I've given it up.

GEMMA: Really?

RORY: Yeah. Six months sober.

GEMMA: So miracles really do happen.

Beat.

Sorry.

Beat.

I'm proud of you.

RORY: Not a lot of answers at the bottom of a bottle.

GEMMA: Not a lot of answers anywhere.

Pause.

RORY: How's your mum?

GEMMA: Old. Waiting. Impatiently.

RORY: What for?

GEMMA: The end.

RORY: Good to see she's still of the same disposition as I remember her.

GEMMA: She still asks after you.

RORY: Yeah?

GEMMA: Yeah.

RORY: Still wishing me dead?

GEMMA: Only in her lucid moments.

He laughs.

RORY: I'm sorry.

GEMMA: Don't be.

RORY: My old man passed away last year.

GEMMA: I heard. Sounded like some wake.

RORY: RNLI.

GEMMA: Saving lives and drinking pints.

RORY: Something like that.

GEMMA: What was it?

RORY: Pneumonia. They reckon the fluid built up over time in his lungs.

GEMMA: Like drowning?

RORY: In a way.

GEMMA: All those years. Mr fucking action hero out on the boat. And that's how it ends. Drowning. In an armchair.

RORY: He knew it was coming. Stopped answering the phone. The door –

GEMMA: You were / speaking?

RORY: The carers told me. Took himself off like a sick dog and went out on his own terms. Something to be said about that.

Pause.

GEMMA: He was an awful cunt, your father.

RORY: GEMMA.

GEMMA: He was.

RORY: You don't get to say that about other people's families.

GEMMA: Nearly mine.

RORY: Nearly.

Beat.

I'd have ruined it anyway. It's what I do.

GEMMA: Been nice to have the chance though.

RORY: Yeah. Yeah, it would.

Pause.

GEMMA: It's not fair.

Beat.

Suppose not much is though.

Pause.

RORY: I've tried to be a better person since it happened. You know, think of other people. But in the end you might as well not bother. You might as well just do what I did when I was seventeen. Just take. Don't get bloody caught though. Do what the fuck you want and don't get caught. Because there's not some fucking scale that we're judged on. Some bloke at the pearly gates. The good people don't get a better life and the cunts a shit one. There's just this. And then it's over. Some longer, some quicker, some painful, some in a fucking armchair. There's no fair.

GEMMA: Some just standing in the wrong place by the side of a road.

A silence.

RORY: Yeah.

Beat.

Never think it's going to be like that do you? Tragedy. Not tragedy... Horror. Just something mundane. All those things you worry about. All those nightmares running through your head when they're young. And then it's just the everyday. That's where it really is. And it's quiet, isn't it? Quiet and lonely. That's what real horror is.

A silence.

GEMMA: She hated buses.

RORY: She did.

GEMMA: Would have pissed her right off.

RORY: Fuming. She would be fuming.

GEMMA: Wouldn't be happy about the moping you've been doing either.

RORY: Me?

GEMMA: I have my spies.

RORY: People have been calling you the black widow of Mersea.

GEMMA: Not to my face.

RORY: They never do round here, do they?

Beat.

Saw the for-sale sign outside your place.

GEMMA: Yeah?

A silence.

Say something.

RORY: Something.

GEMMA: That's not funny.

Pause.

RORY: Where?

GEMMA: Clacton.

RORY: Blackpool of the South.

GEMMA: Fancied a change. Nothing left to keep me here is there anymore.

Pause.

RORY: Will you get a good price?

GEMMA: Yeah.

RORY: Cowboys all them estate agents. I could have come round and –

GEMMA: Money doesn't matter, Rory. None of it fucking matters.

A silence.

RORY: I'm happy for you. You deserve it. A fresh start.

GEMMA: Don't think we get fresh starts at our age.

RORY: Change of scenery then. That's something.

GEMMA: And you?

RORY: I'll be staying. Where would I go?

Beat.

They reckon I'll be running the caravan site when the old boy retires.

GEMMA: That's good.

RORY: It is what it is.

GEMMA: I'm glad you found something.

GEMMA *takes out another cigarette.*

RORY: Fucking chimney on you.

She lights it.

GEMMA: I'm the one who called the police. I didn't think your dad would press charges.

Pause.

I wanted to tell you. Always have.

Beat.

No better time than when you're running away is there. To tell someone the truth.

A moment.

If I hadn't. If you had just –

RORY: No point in thinking about ifs. Wasted seventeen years doing that.

Beat.

If I'd just given her a lift.

GEMMA: You were over the limit.

RORY: If I wasn't such a fucking drunk. If for once in my life I was just –

GEMMA: It was an accident, Rory. An accident. No one's fault.

A long silence.

RORY: I stole the money for you. For us.

GEMMA: Didn't feel like it as you were walking out that door.

RORY: If you'd have just told me about –

GEMMA: You'd have stayed?

Pause.

I was a kid, Rory. Pregnant. I didn't even know if you'd want to…

She stops herself.

RORY: Of course I would.

A silence.

GEMMA: I wanted to visit you.

RORY: I was there three years.

GEMMA: I know.

RORY: That's a lot of time

GEMMA: It didn't feel like it.

RORY: It did to me.

GEMMA: It's unforgivable.

RORY: Is that why you avoided me when I got out?

A silence.

GEMMA: You missed her when she was a baby. You missed…

RORY: Would have been rubbish at it anyway. Probably done her a favour.

GEMMA: I don't think so.

RORY: You did a good job.

GEMMA: I had my moments.

RORY: Bet she did too.

GEMMA: Oh you can imagine.

RORY: I can.

He moves to her and holds her.

A very long moment.

GEMMA: I never took a turn that night.

RORY: A turn of what?

GEMMA: A story.

RORY: What are you talking about?

GEMMA: Halloween. You with your candles and pumpkins.

Beat.

RORY: Pumpkin. Singular.

GEMMA: I've got one. Now. A ghost story. If you'd like to hear it.

RORY: Prepared it just in case, did you?

GEMMA: Was bound to bump into you sooner or later.

RORY: Shame it had to be here.

GEMMA: Feels pretty apt to me.

Pause.

RORY: Go on then.

She takes a breath.

GEMMA: One day, and this wasn't a remarkable day or anything, just a day… A woman woke up and went downstairs in her house. She put on the kettle like she always did. Took out a mug and started to make a coffee. Then her bowl of muesli from the fridge. Just like she does on any other morning. She sits down. But she just can't seem to lift the spoon up off the table. And the coffee. It just sits there too. Without so much as a sip taken from it. The alarm on her phone goes off and tells her that she needs to leave to get to work on time.

RORY: She's one of those people is she. With the phone alarms.

GEMMA: Yeah. Can't function without them. But today. Today she just keeps on sitting there. And the coffee goes cold. And the muesli gets warm. And she just sits there. Watching the clock. And she stays like that. Till the exact minute she is meant to start her job. The exact second her shift is meant to start. Then she stands. And she leaves the house. She walks calmly and methodically in the direction of the Strood.

RORY: Gemma…

GEMMA: I say in the direction. But really it's far enough away from her house that you wouldn't know if you saw her.

It takes her about forty minutes. At a steady pace. She is starting to sweat. Even though it's not a particularly warm day. She can feel it. Behind her knees. And under her arms. And she is not a woman who sweats. Not normally. She notices that the tide has already started to come in.

RORY *takes out a cigarette. Lights it.*

She approaches the Strood. And sees that, as usual, there are a couple of cars there. A couple of people caught out. She walks past them. And now the water is starting to lap at her feet. A coldness to it. And she bends down and takes off her shoes. And now she can feel the tarmac. The road. On her bare feet. She can feel it. And she just continues to walk into the water. And soon it's up to her ankles. Then her knees. And then the hem of her dress. And she's sure that the people in the cars behind her are wondering what the fuck she is doing. As the water is almost at her waist now. And it's not every day you watch a middle-aged woman walk into the water fully clothed. But by now she doesn't care. By now she is nearly halfway across. And the water covers her shoulders. Her neck. Her…

And I stop.

She stops.

RORY *is crying. Silently.*

When she gets to work no one even notices her dress is wet. They don't notice she's late. Maybe someone sees a damp patch on the carpet later on. But they don't know it's her. They don't see her. No one does. And that night she goes home. And she finds the cup of cold coffee sat there on the table. Just where she left it. With the muesli next to it.

And then she goes to bed. And she lies down. And it meant nothing. None of it. None of it meant a thing.

And she lies there thinking that. That exact thought. Till eventually the darkness of night makes her drift off to sleep.

A silence.

RORY: That's not a ghost story.

GEMMA: Yes. It is.

A long silence.

RORY: She'd have been happy wouldn't she?

GEMMA: She was happy.

RORY: You know what I mean.

GEMMA: I think she would.

RORY: Happier than us.

GEMMA: Not exactly setting the bar high are we.

RORY: For a time though.

GEMMA: Yeah. For a time.

A silence.

GEMMA: I better be getting back. Ran out of fags and everything.

RORY: I can spot you one.

GEMMA: Nah, two packets in a day are enough for me.

RORY: This was…

GEMMA: Nice?

He smiles.

RORY: Yes. Yes it was.

Pause.

Good luck with the move

GEMMA: Thanks.

A moment.

If I stayed…

RORY: Don't.

GEMMA: I could –

RORY: No.

A moment.

GEMMA: No?

RORY: No.

GEMMA: I didn't mean –

RORY: It's fine, Gemma.

A longer moment.

GEMMA: I just…

She takes his hand.

It doesn't matter.

A moment.

RORY: Shall we?

GEMMA: You escorting me home?

RORY: I'll walk you to the corner.

GEMMA: Wouldn't want my mum seeing.

RORY: Or your sister.

GEMMA: A jealous harlot at the best of times.

RORY: And then later?

Beat.

GEMMA: I'll meet you down the lifeboat station.

RORY: We breaking in?

GEMMA: Course we're fucking breaking in.

RORY: Don't want to go to the pub?

GEMMA: Nah. I'm not drinking.

RORY: No?

GEMMA: No.

RORY: What do you want to do instead?

He gives a her a look. She smiles.

GEMMA: Yeah, you'll be lucky.

RORY: Gotta be one of these days ain't I?

GEMMA: Yeah.

RORY: No ghost stories?

GEMMA: Not this time.

A silence.

RORY: You know sometimes… If I listen hard enough… I swear… I can still hear her voice.

Beat.

It's not so bad here, is it?

GEMMA *starts to exit.*

GEMMA: You coming?

RORY: I'll catch you up.

She smiles at him. Exits.

He takes one more look at the flowers and cards.

The sound of the waves lapping over The Strood can be heard. The tide rising.

He doesn't move.

We wait.

The sound of the waves is getting louder.

He doesn't move.

We wait…

Blackout.

www.salamanderstreet.com